# THE NORDIC REGION

# SWEDEN

MICHELLE LOMBERG

www.openlightbox.com

## Step 1
Go to **www.openlightbox.com**

## Step 2
Enter this unique code

**ZYNBA4Q8D**

## Step 3
Explore your interactive eBook!

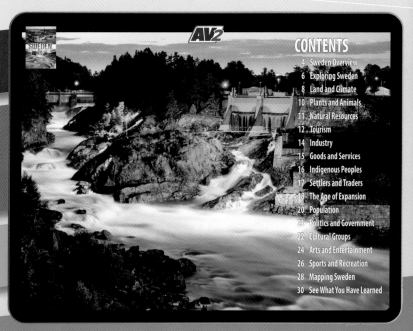

### CONTENTS

**AV2 is optimized for use on any device**

# Your interactive eBook comes with...

**Contents**
Browse a live contents page to easily navigate through resources

**Audio**
Listen to sections of the book read aloud

**Videos**
Watch informative video clips

**Weblinks**
Gain additional information for research

**Slideshows**
View images and captions

**Try This!**
Complete activities and hands-on experiments

**Key Words**
Study vocabulary, and complete a matching word activity

**Quizzes**
Test your knowledge

**Share**
Share titles within your Learning Management System (LMS) or Library Circulation System

**Citation**
Create bibliographical references following APA, CMOS, and MLA styles

# This title is part of our AV2 digital subscription

**1-Year 3–8 Subscription**
ISBN 978-1-7911-3306-1

Access hundreds of AV2 titles with our digital subscription.
Sign up for a FREE trial at **www.openlightbox.com/trial**

# THE NORDIC REGION
# SWEDEN

# Contents

# Sweden Overview

The country of Sweden is located on the Scandinavian **Peninsula** in northeastern Europe. Its northern location gives Sweden a cold climate compared to many other nations. Abundant natural resources and high-tech industries help make Sweden a wealthy country. Its citizens enjoy good schools, high-quality health care, and a high standard of living. Most people in Sweden can buy the products and services they need to live well.

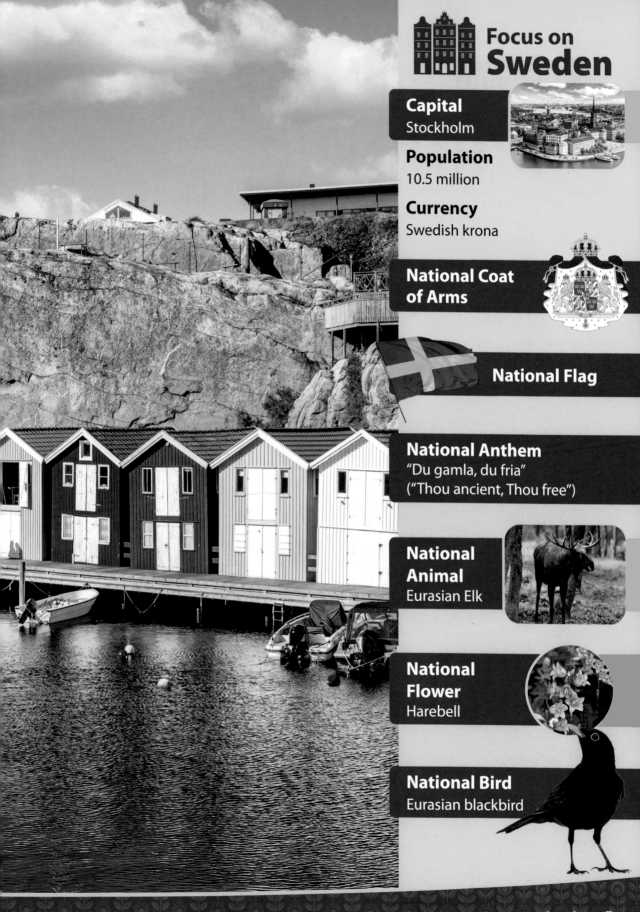

## Focus on Sweden

**Capital**
Stockholm

**Population**
10.5 million

**Currency**
Swedish krona

**National Coat of Arms**

**National Flag**

**National Anthem**
"Du gamla, du fria"
("Thou ancient, Thou free")

**National Animal**
Eurasian Elk

**National Flower**
Harebell

**National Bird**
Eurasian blackbird

# Exploring Sweden

Sweden has an area of 173,860 square miles (450,295 square kilometers). It occupies the eastern part of the Scandinavian Peninsula. The country of Norway covers the western portion of the peninsula and borders Sweden to the west. Finland borders Sweden to the north, and the Baltic Sea and Gulf of Bothnia lie to Sweden's east. To the southwest and south, three **straits** separate Sweden from Denmark. Sweden, Norway, and Denmark are often referred to as the Scandinavian countries.

## Stockholm

Stockholm is Sweden's capital and largest city. It was first settled in the 13th century. Much of the city is built on islands in Lake Mälaren, near the Baltic coast.

## Mount Kebne

Located in northern Sweden, Mount Kebne is the country's highest mountain. It stands 6,926 feet (2,111 meters) tall. Snow and ice cover the peak year-round.

## Lake Vänern

Lake Vänern, or Väner, is Sweden's largest lake. It covers 2,181 square miles (5,650 sq. km). Parts of the lake are 348 feet (106 m) deep.

## Dalälven River

The Dalälven is the longest river located entirely in Sweden. The waterway extends for 323 miles (520 km). It flows into the Gulf of Bothnia.

# Land and Climate

S weden is a long, narrow country. It extends about 1,000 miles (1,600 km) from north to south and 300 miles (480 km) from east to west. The land is mountainous, especially in western Sweden. Areas near the country's east and south coast are at lower **elevation**. Rivers flow from the mountains toward the coast. The long, mostly rocky coastline features many **inlets** and small islands. Throughout the country, there are thousands of lakes.

Sweden has three geographic regions. From north to south, they are Norrland, Svealand, and Götaland. Norrland is the largest and most mountainous region.

Much of Norrland lies north of the Arctic Circle. In this region, the Sun never sets in the summer days around June 21. During the winter, there is no daylight in the period around December 21. Norrland's climate is cold and dry. In summer, temperatures are about 68 degrees Fahrenheit (20 degrees Celsius).

Like all of Lapland's rivers, the Abiskojokk originates in glaciers found high in Sweden's western mountains. Known as the Kamajokk at higher elevations, the river runs for 25 miles (40 km) before emptying into Lake Torneträsk.

Svealand, in central Sweden, is the country's smallest region. It includes highlands in the west and **fertile** plains in the east. Svealand has a warmer climate than Norrland, but winters are still snowy and cold. January temperatures are often below 32°F (0°C).

Götaland, the southernmost region, has large areas of plains. Sandy beaches line some of the area's coast. Götaland has a fairly mild climate because of the **Gulf Stream**. Snow is rare in Götaland, and summer temperatures can range from 59°F (15°C) to 77°F (25°C).

Sweden's far north is also part of an area called Lapland. This region spreads across northern Norway, Sweden, and Finland, as well as the Kola Peninsula in Russia. It is named for the Sami, or Lapp, people. They have lived in the area for thousands of years.

# Seasonal Sweden

## Temperature (Average Highs)

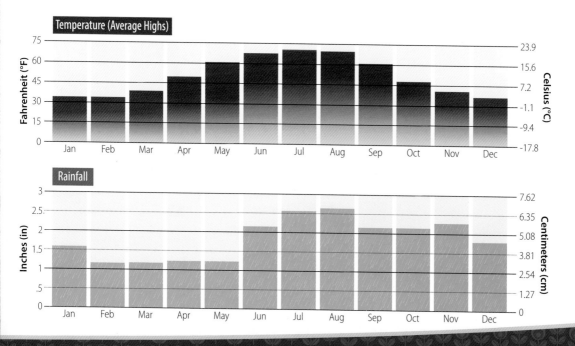

| | Fahrenheit (°F) | Celsius (°C) |
|---|---|---|

75 — 23.9
60 — 15.6
45 — 7.2
30 — -1.1
15 — -9.4
0 — -17.8

Jan Feb Mar Apr May Jun Jul Aug Sep Oct Nov Dec

## Rainfall

Inches (in) — Centimeters (cm)

3 — 7.62
2.5 — 6.35
2 — 5.08
1.5 — 3.81
1 — 2.54
.5 — 1.27
0 — 0

Jan Feb Mar Apr May Jun Jul Aug Sep Oct Nov Dec

# Plants and Animals

**M**uch of Sweden is covered by forests. Fir, pine, and birch trees are common throughout the country. Beech, oak, elm, and maple trees also thrive in southern Sweden. Twinflower plants are found on the forest floor. Their white or pink flowers grow in pairs from long stems. Blueberry and lingonberry bushes grow well in forested areas.

🇸🇪 Lingonberries are often served as a condiment, adding to the flavor of many traditional Swedish dishes.

Brown bears, lynx, and wolves live in the northern forests. Reindeer roam lowland areas in the north. The Sami people use reindeer for food and to pull sleds or wagons.

Eurasian elk, or moose, are common in all regions of Sweden. The world's largest type of deer, moose can grow to be about 7 feet (2.1 m) tall and weigh up to 1,875 pounds (850 kilograms). A male's antlers can extend 6 feet (1.8 m) from end to end. Most moose have dark brown or black fur. White moose, which are rare, are also sometimes seen in Sweden.

🇸🇪 Sweden's wolf population sits at about 400. The animals are found mainly in the north-central part of the country.

🇸🇪 Sweden has more moose per square mile (2.6 square km) than any other country in the world.

# Natural Resources

Sweden is rich in natural resources, including its forests. Wood from the country's forests is used to produce lumber. Leftover scraps from lumber production, known as biomass, are burned to heat buildings or generate electricity.

Many of Sweden's rivers are used to produce hydroelectricity. This is electricity created from the energy of moving water. A dam on a river directs water through machines called turbines, making them spin. The spinning causes generators connected to the turbines to create electricity. Most of the country's hydroelectricity is produced in northern Sweden.

The Göta Älv River has a drop of about 105 feet (32 meters) near the town of Trollhättan. The force of this falling water is used to power two power stations.

A variety of minerals are mined in Sweden. The northern part of the country has large deposits of iron ore, copper, lead, zinc, and gold. The mine at Kiruna, in the far north, is the world's largest underground iron ore mine. Gold and other metals are also mined in Svealand.

While the iron ore bed found at Kiruna extends approximately 1.25 miles (2 km) into the ground, the mining itself has only progressed to a depth of about 0.8 miles (1.3 km).

# Tourism

Sweden's natural beauty, historic sites, and modern culture attract visitors from elsewhere in Europe and around the world. Almost 2 million people visited Sweden in 2020. They spent a total of more than $4 billion.

In 1909, Sweden became the first country in Europe to establish national parks. Today, the country has 30 national parks. Visitors to these protected areas can enjoy the beauty of Sweden's diverse **habitats**, including mountains, lakes, forests, and seacoasts. The newest park, Åsnen, opened in 2018. It is made up of more than 1,000 islands.

Tourists interested in history can take a ferry to the island of Gotland. The town of Visby, on Gotland, has many buildings that date back to the **Middle Ages**, when Visby was a major trading center. A museum provides a history of Visby, which is a **UNESCO** World Heritage site.

Sweden has many other museums, including Stockholm's Moderna Museet. Its collection features paintings, sculptures, drawings, photographs, and other artworks created in the 20th and 21st centuries. The museum also has a branch in the city of Malmö. In Göteborg, the Göteborgs Konstmuseum is one of the country's largest art museums. It displays artworks created from the 15th century to the present day. Paintings by some of Europe's best-known artists, including Rembrandt van Rijn and Pablo Picasso, are on display.

Visby's medieval history is on display in the area known as the "old town," where up to 200 buildings dating from the 12th to 14th centuries remain.

Liseberg has been offering its visitors fun and games since 1923. Today, it welcomes approximately 3.1 million guests annually.

Visitors to the city of Uppsala can visit the Linnaeus Museum and its garden. The museum is in the former home of 18th-century scientist Carolus, or Carl, Linnaeus. He developed a system of classifying animals and plants based on their features that is still largely used today. The museum displays items related to Linnaeus's research, including the cabinets where he kept his herb and insect collections. The garden around the museum is maintained by Uppsala University. The types of plants in the garden were all grown by Linnaeus during his lifetime.

Thrill seekers enjoy the Liseberg amusement park in Göteborg. The park has about 40 rides, including the Helix. This is a rollercoaster that travels at more than 60 miles (100 km) per hour. The park also stages rock music concerts.

# Industry

Sweden's **gross domestic product** (GDP) in 2021 was about $627 billion. Manufacturing and other industries that provide products, such as forestry and mining, account for almost one quarter of the country's GDP. About 18 percent of Swedish workers have jobs in these industries.

The Volvo plant in Torslanda produces approximately 300,000 cars per year.

Some manufacturing is related to the country's natural resources. Factories make paper, furniture, and other wood products from trees cut down in Sweden's forests. Steel is manufactured using iron from Swedish mines.

Motor vehicle manufacturing is a major Swedish industry. Volvo cars, trucks, buses, and construction equipment are made in Sweden. Scania is a company that produces trucks and buses. High-tech products made in Sweden include communications equipment and other electronics. The manufacturing of medications and other medical products is increasing as well.

Agriculture is not a major industry because only a small portion of the land in Sweden is suitable for farming. Major crops grown on this land include wheat, barley, potatoes, and vegetables. Some farmers raise cows for their milk.

## Sweden GDP by Sector

Sweden's GDP can be separated into three main sectors. Service-related industries are the top contributor. The country's economy also benefits from product-driven industries and agriculture.

**74.3%**
**Services**

**24.2%**
**Industry**

**1.5%**
**Agriculture**

# Goods and Services

Service industries drive Sweden's economy. People in these industries provide services to others rather than produce goods. Service workers are employed in government offices, schools, hospitals, stores, hotels, and restaurants.

Trade with other nations is important to Sweden's economy. In many industries, **exports** account for a large portion of total sales. Leading Swedish exports include paper and wood products, motor vehicles, and machinery.

IKEA is one of the best-known names in home furnishings. The company was founded in Sweden in 1943.

Sweden **imports** a variety of products, including goods it cannot produce in large amounts. Many types of food items are imported. The country also imports petroleum, or oil, that it needs for fuel.

In 1995, Sweden became a member of the **European Union (EU)**. Today, much of the country's trade is with other EU nations. These countries include Germany, Norway, Denmark, and the Netherlands.

Export goods are often packed in large containers for shipping. At Göteborg and other ports, large cranes are used to lift the containers on to ships.

# Indigenous Peoples

People have lived in Sweden for at least 11,000 years. Before then, during the last **Ice Age**, the area was covered by large sheets of ice. As the climate became warmer and the ice began to melt, people moved into Sweden from other regions. Some groups probably traveled from present-day Denmark. They survived by fishing, hunting, and gathering plants for food.

The Sami considered knives an essential tool and took great pride in crafting them. They would often carve the handles of their knives from reindeer antlers.

The Sami may have reached Sweden from Russia about 10,000 years ago. Traditional Sami society was organized into family groups called *siida*. Some *siida* lived in permanent settlements. Others were nomadic, moving from place to place in search of food.

Often, the oldest person in a *siida* was the group's leader. Another important person in a *siida* was a man called the *noaidi*. People believed he could predict the future, cure illnesses, and communicate with the gods the Sami worshipped.

The Sami lived in huts called *goahtis* for much of the year, and then used tent-like structures called *lavvus* when migrating with the reindeer. Each type of home was built around a central fire.

# Settlers and Traders

Over the centuries, new groups of settlers reached Sweden from elsewhere in Europe. By about 2,500 BC, farming communities had developed in southern Sweden. People in these communities grew crops and raised cattle.

By 1,500 BC, people were using bronze, made from copper and tin, for tools, weapons, and ornaments. They traded with areas farther south in Europe. To honor the dead, people in southern Sweden used **megaliths** to mark burial mounds and other grave sites. Petroglyphs, or carvings on rock, have also been found at some graves.

Gotland Island is home to numerous picture stones, some dating back as far as 400 AD. Historians believe that the images on the stones are religious in nature.

In about 500 BC, during a period of history known as the Iron Age, people in Sweden began to use iron instead of bronze for tools and weapons. Iron tools are stronger than those made from bronze. By the 1st century AD, trade expanded with other parts of Europe, including areas controlled by the Roman Empire. Two powerful groups developed at this time. They were the Götar, in southern Sweden, and the Svear, in the region now called Svealand.

One of Sweden's best-known megalithic monuments is the Ale's Stones, found near the town of Ystad. The 59 stones appear to be placed in the shape of a ship, but their actual purpose is unknown.

# The Age of Expansion

Beginning in about 800 AD, warriors from Sweden, as well as Norway and Denmark, set sail for other parts of Europe and beyond. These warriors, known as Vikings, staged raids to capture valuable goods. They also tried to conquer land and control trade with other regions.

Most of Sweden's Vikings explored to the east and southeast. They first crossed the Baltic Sea to Russia. Then, they sailed Russia's rivers to the Black Sea and Constantinople, the present-day city of Istanbul, Turkey.

By the 11th century, Viking power had declined. It was at about this time that **missionaries** from other parts of Europe brought Christianity to Sweden. The Swedish king, Olaf, tried to control the entire country. However, for the next several centuries, there were many conflicts between Swedish leaders, as well as wars with Denmark and Norway.

Powerful Swedish kings gained control of most of present-day Sweden by the 1500s. In the 1600s, Sweden tried to establish **colonies** on other continents. In North America, the New Sweden colony included several settlements along the Delaware River, in parts of today's Delaware, New Jersey, and Pennsylvania. The largest settlement was Fort Christina, at the site of what is now Wilmington, Delaware. However, few people moved to the area, and the colony was soon captured by the Dutch.

Between 1650 and 1663, Sweden set up several settlements along the coast of present-day Ghana, in western Africa. Swedish merchants traded with local peoples to obtain both gold and slaves. The slaves were then sent to North or South America to be sold. The Swedish colony eventually fell to the Dutch.

In the mid-1600s, Sweden also expanded the area it controlled in northern Europe. King Charles X Gustaf led the nation in a successful war against Denmark in 1657. Sweden gained land as a result of the war, establishing the modern-day boundaries of the country.

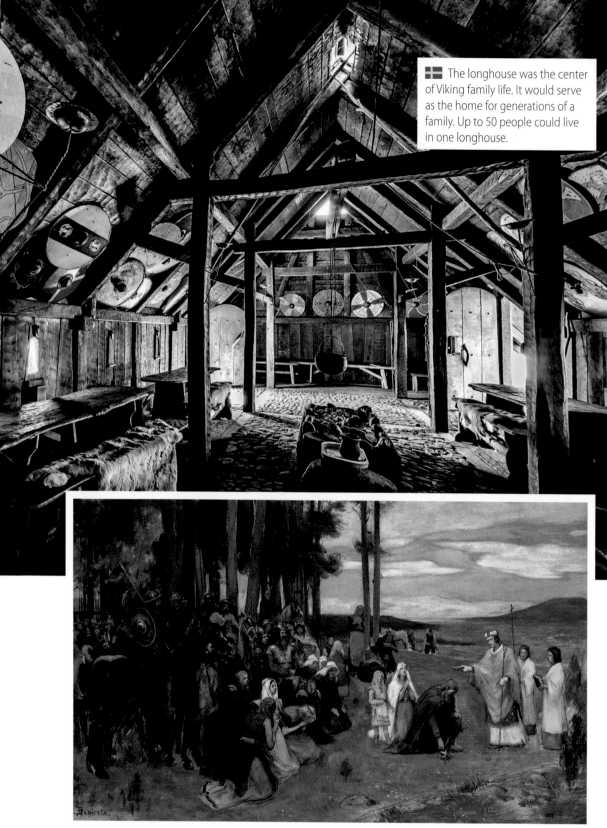

The longhouse was the center of Viking family life. It would serve as the home for generations of a family. Up to 50 people could live in one longhouse.

Ansgar, a Benedictine monk, was the first missionary to arrive in Sweden, in about 829 AD. He was later named the patron saint of Scandinavia for bringing Christianity to the Nordic region.

# Population

About 10.5 million people call Sweden home. Most Swedes live in the southern part of the country, where the climate is warmer. Overall, Sweden is not densely populated. On average, the country has 67 people per square mile (26 people per sq. km). This compares to 94 people per square mile (36 people per sq. km) in the United States.

More than 88 percent of Sweden's population lives in **urban** areas. Stockholm has a population of about 1.7 million. The second-largest city, Göteborg, has more than 620,000 people. Approximately 330,000 people live in Malmö.

About 20 percent of Sweden's people were born in another country. Some of these **immigrants** have moved from nearby European nations, such as Finland or Poland. In recent years, tens of thousands of people have traveled to Sweden from Syria, Iraq, and other countries in the Middle East or Africa. Many of the immigrants were fleeing wars in their homelands.

Besides having a warmer climate, southern communities also give people easy access to mainland Europe. Malmö, for instance, sits just across the Öresund Strait from Copenhagen, the capital of Denmark.

### Sweden Age Groups

Like many highly developed countries, Sweden has an aging population and a low birth rate. Most of its citizens are currently of working age. The country's **median age** is 41.1.

**17.7%**
**Age 0–14 years**

**61.8%**
**Age 15–64 years**

**20.5%**
**Age 65+ years**

# Politics and Government

S weden has a type of government called a constitutional monarchy. A king or queen is the head of state, or highest-level government official. However, in recent times, the monarch's powers have become very limited. Officials elected by the people largely run the government. This makes Sweden a democracy.

Sweden has an elected Parliament, or legislature, that passes the country's laws. In the Swedish language, the Parliament is called the Riksdag. Typically, the leader of the political party with the most seats in the Riksdag is named by the king or queen to be the country's prime minister.

The prime minister is the head of the government. He or she appoints a cabinet. This is a group of officials who advise the prime minister and head various government departments, such as education or relations with other countries. The prime minister and cabinet members propose new laws to the Riksdag and make sure existing laws are followed.

Ulf Kristersson became Sweden's prime minister in 2022. He is the 35th person to hold the position.

One of the key duties of King Carl XVI Gustaf, and other Swedish monarchs, is to open Parliament. The ceremony is typically accompanied by much fanfare, with horse-drawn carriages and military processions.

# Cultural Groups

**M**ost people in Sweden today have Swedish **ancestry**. Other cultural groups include the Sami and people with Finnish ancestry. The Tornedalers are a Finnish people who have lived for centuries in the region around the Torne River.

Jewish people began to settle in Sweden in the late 18th century. Today, approximately 15,000 Jews call Sweden home. The country's largest Jewish community is in Stockholm. The first **Roma** arrived in Sweden 500 years ago. The Swedish Roma population today is about 50,000.

The official language of Sweden is Swedish. Many people in Sweden learn English in school. Sami, Finnish, Meänkieli, Yiddish, and Romani are all official minority languages. Yiddish is spoken by many European Jews. Romani is the language of the Roma people. Meänkieli is a **dialect** of Finnish spoken by the Tornedalers.

The most common religion in Sweden is Lutheranism, a Christian faith. It became the country's official religion in 1544, and remained so for more than 450 years. Until 1952, all Swedish citizens were required to belong to the Church of Sweden, which follows Lutheranism. As of the year 2000, Sweden no longer has an official religion.

Today, a number of other religions are practiced in Sweden. They include Christian faiths besides Lutheranism, as well as Judaism and Islam, the religion of Muslims. The number of Muslims in Sweden has grown in recent years as immigration from the Middle East, where most people practice Islam, has increased. About one-third of the people in Sweden do not follow any religion.

While many Sami now live a modern lifestyle, they continue to keep their traditional ways alive in many ways. Reindeer races pay tribute to the past, when the Sami would meet to test the speed of their reindeer before they led the animals on their spring migration.

🇸🇪 Uppsala Cathedral serves as the base for the Archbishop of Uppsala, the leader of the Church of Sweden. Until 1719, it was where most of the country's monarchs were crowned. Today, Sweden's royal family often attends services there.

# Arts and Entertainment

Sweden's creative artists include writers, musicians, movie directors, and actors who are well known around the world. The government supports the arts through the Swedish Arts Council. This organization provides money to help creative artists develop or perform works of literature, music, and dance.

Books by Swedish writers are popular worldwide and have been translated into dozens of languages. Astrid Lindgren is one of Sweden's best-known authors. She wrote a series of children's books about the adventures of Pippi Longstocking, a red-haired and extremely strong girl who often misbehaves.

Adult readers enjoy the works of Swedish authors such as Stieg Larsson. His novel *The Girl with the Dragon Tattoo* was made into an award-winning 2011 film. Henning Mankell wrote a series of crime novels featuring police detective Kurt Wallander. The popular television series *Wallander* is based on Mankell's books.

Swedish movie directors and actors are also known around the world. Ingmar Bergman directed and wrote dozens of films. His 1982 movie *Fanny and Alexander* won an Academy Award for best foreign-language film. Director Lasse Hallström's movies include *What's Eating Gilbert Grape*, *The Cider House Rules,* and *Chocolat*. Well-known Swedish actors include Ingrid Bergman. From 1945 to 1975, she won three Academy Awards for best actress or best supporting actress. Alicia Vikander has appeared in dozens of films. She won a 2016 best supporting actress Academy Award for her role in *The Danish Girl*.

ABBA has sold more than 200 million albums worldwide.

🇩🇰 The first *Battlefield* video game launched in 2002. Since then, DICE has developed 13 other games in the series. The most recent, *Battlefield 2042*, was released in 2021.

The pop-music group ABBA is one of the most successful bands of recent decades. Its four members began performing together in the 1970s and achieved worldwide fame. Their music was the basis of the play and movie *Mamma Mia!* Other popular Swedish recording artists include The Hives, Robyn, Tove Lo, and Zara Larsson.

Swedish developers have produced some of the world's most successful games. Stockholm-based DICE is the creator of *Battlefield*. Mojang, also in Stockholm, is the creator of *Minecraft*. King, with studios in Sweden and around the world, produces more than 180 games, including *Candy Crush Saga*.

# Sports

People in Sweden take part in many types of sports. About 3 million Swedes belong to a sports club. Members of these clubs enjoy a variety of activities, including skiing, golf, ice hockey, and handball. The most popular sport is soccer, which is called football in Sweden.

Long Scandinavian winters allow Swedes to excel at winter sports. Magdalena Forsberg is considered one of the best women's **biathlon** athletes to ever compete for the country. She stepped onto the World Cup podium more than 70 times.

Ingemar Stenmark is one of the most successful alpine, or downhill, skiers in the history of the sport. In the 1970s and 1980s, he won a record 86 World Cup races, competing in the **slalom** and giant slalom. Stenmark won gold medals in both slalom events at the 1980 Winter Olympics.

Ice hockey star Peter Forsberg played both on the Swedish national team and in North America's National Hockey League (NHL). Forsberg helped the national team win two Olympic gold medals, in 1994 and 2006. He was a member of the Colorado Avalanche team that won two NHL championships, in 1996 and 2001.

Sweden's biggest cross-country ski race is the Vasaloppet. The race honors a journey taken by Swedish leader Gustaf Eriksson Vasa in 1520 during his struggle against Denmark. Today, the 57-mile (90-km) Vasaloppet race retraces his route from Sären to Mora.

In addition to winter sports, many Swedes enjoy traditional sports and games of the region. Varpa and kubb have been played since Viking times. In varpa, players throw a heavy disk, called the varpa, toward a pin in the ground about 11 to 22 yards (10 to 20 m) away. Players take 36 turns, with the distance between the varpa and the pin measured each time. The player with the smallest total distance wins. Kubb is played by teams of 2 to 12 players. Rectangular wooden blocks called kubbs, along with a larger block called the king, are arranged on the field of play. Teams take turns throwing batons, with the aim of knocking over the kubbs without toppling the king.

🇸🇪 Sweden placed sixth at the 2022 Winter Olympics in Beijing, China, with a total of 18 medals. Jonna Sundling was one of the country's gold medalists, winning the women's sprint in cross-country skiing.

🇸🇪 Today, kubb's reach has extended past Sweden's borders. The game is now played in other European countries as well as the United States and Canada.

# Mapping Sweden

We use many tools to interpret maps and to understand the locations of features such as cities, states, lakes, and rivers. The map below has many tools to help interpret information on the map of Sweden.

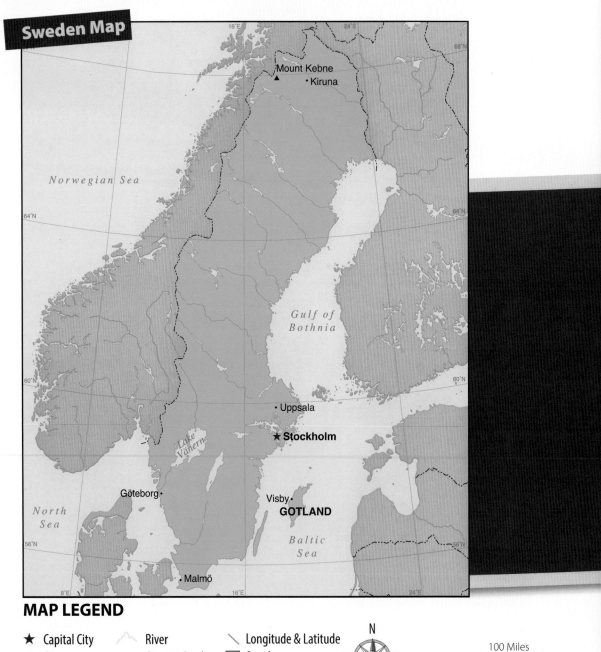

**Sweden Map**

## MAP LEGEND

★ Capital City
● City
🗺 Body of Water

⌒ River
·–·· Country Border
▲ Mountain

╲ Longitude & Latitude
▨ Sweden
▨ Other Countries

N
W ✦ E    SCALE
S

100 Miles
100 Km

## Mapping Tools

- The compass rose shows north, south, east, and west. The points in-between represent northeast, northwest, southeast, and southwest.

- The map scale shows that the distances on a map represent much longer distances in real life. If you measure the distance between objects on a map, you can use the map scale to calculate the actual distance in miles or kilometers between those two points.

- The lines of latitude and longitude are long lines that appear on maps. The lines of latitude run east to west and measure how far north or south of the equator a place is located. The lines of longitude run north to south and measure how far east or west of the Prime Meridian a place is located. A location on a map can be found by using the two numbers where latitude and longitude meet. This number is called a coordinate and is written using degrees and direction. For example, the city of Stockholm would be found at 59°N and 18°E on a map.

# Map It!

## Using the map and the appropriate tools, complete the activities below.

### Locating with latitude and longitude
1. Which body of water is located at 59°N and 13°E?
2. Which island is located at 57°N and 18°E
3. Which city is located at 55°N and 13°E?

### Distances between points
4. Using the map scale and a ruler, calculate the approximate distance between Stockholm and Kiruna.
5. Using the map scale and a ruler, calculate the approximate distance between Uppsala and Stockholm.
6. Using the map scale and a ruler, calculate the approximate distance between Göteborg and Malmö.

Swed

# See What You Have Learned

Test your knowledge of Sweden by answering these questions.

**1** What is the capital of Sweden?

**2** How many official minority languages does Sweden have?

**3** Which cultural group speaks Meänkieli?

**4** Which type of animal is most associated with the Sami people?

**5** What is the name of Sweden's biggest cross-country skiing race?

**6** Which town on the island of Gotland is a UNESCO World Heritage Site?

**7** What type of government does Sweden have?

**8** Which Swedish gaming company created *Minecraft*?

**9** Which Swedish town has the world's largest underground iron ore mine?

**10** About how many people live in Sweden?

# Key Words

**ancestry:** referring to people in one's family or cultural group in past times

**biathlon:** a sport that involves both cross-country skiing and target shooting

**colonies:** countries or areas controlled by foreign country

**dialect:** a form of a language spoken in a certain area or by a specific group of people

**elevation:** the height of an area of land above sea level

**European Union (EU):** a political and economic organization, established in 1993, that has more than two dozen member countries

**exports:** goods sold to other countries

**fertile:** referring to land that is suitable for growing crops or other plants

**gross domestic product:** the total value of goods and services produced in a country or area

**Gulf Stream:** a current of warm water that flows from the Caribbean region across the Atlantic Ocean to northern Europe

**habitats:** types of natural areas and the plants and animals that live in them

**Ice Age:** a long period of time when Earth's climate is especially cold

**immigrants:** people who come to a new country or area to live and work

**imports:** buys goods from other countries

**inlets:** narrow bodies of water that cut into a coastline

**median age:** the age that divides a population into two parts of equal size

**megaliths:** large stones used by ancient peoples for monuments

**Middle Ages:** the period of European history that began in the 5th century and extended to the 13th century

**missionaries:** people who travel to an area to spread a religion

**peninsula:** an area of land surrounded on three sides by water

**Roma:** members of a cultural group that originated in northern India but whose people have largely moved, over the centuries, to Europe and other continents

**slalom:** a type of downhill ski race in which skiers zigzag between sets of poles called gates. In giant slalom races, the gates are farther apart.

**straits:** narrow bodies of water connecting larger bodies of water

**UNESCO:** the United Nations Educational, Scientific, and Cultural Organization, whose main goals are to promote world peace and eliminate poverty through education, science, and culture

**urban:** related to cities and towns

# Index

# Get the best of both worlds.

AV2 bridges the gap between print and digital.

The expandable resources toolbar enables quick access to content including **videos**, **audio**, **activities**, **weblinks**, **slideshows**, **quizzes**, and **key words**.

**Animated videos** make static images come alive.

Resource icons on each page help readers to further **explore key concepts**.

Published by Lightbox Learning Inc.
276 5th Avenue, Suite 704 #917
New York, NY 10001
Website: www.openlightbox.com

Copyright ©2024 Lightbox Learning Inc.
All rights reserved. No part of this publication may be reproduced, stored in a retrieval system, or transmitted in any form or by any means, electronic, mechanical, photocopying, recording, or otherwise, without the prior written permission of the publisher.

Library of Congress Control Number: 2022950707

ISBN 978-1-7911-4724-2 (hardcover)
ISBN 978-1-7911-4725-9 (softcover)
ISBN 978-1-7911-4726-6 (multi-user eBook)

Printed in Guangzhou, China
1 2 3 4 5 6 7 8 9 0   26 25 24 23 22

122021
101322

**Project Coordinator** Heather Kissock
**Designer** Terry Paulhus

**Photo Credits**
Every reasonable effort has been made to trace ownership and to obtain permission to reprint copyright material. The publisher would be pleased to have any errors or omissions brought to its attention so that they may be corrected in subsequent printings. The publisher acknowledges Getty Images, Alamy, Bridgeman Images, Shutterstock, Dreamstime, and Wikimedia as its primary image suppliers for this title.